LUXOR

TRAVEL GUIDE
2025

"Explore The Timeless Allure Of The City Of Eternal Light"

Dennis Pearson

COPYRIGHT © DENNIS PEARSON 2025

All rights reserved. This companion guide, including its content, design, and layout, is protected under international copyright law. No portion of this publication may be reproduced, distributed, or transmitted in any form or by any means whether electronic, mechanical, photocopying, recording, or otherwise without the prior written permission of the author. Unauthorized use or distribution of any material from this guide, including brief quotations in reviews or references, is strictly prohibited and may result in legal action. For permissions, contact the author directly. All inquiries and permissions must be granted in writing. This guide is intended solely for personal use, and any commercial exploitation is expressly forbidden unless specifically authorized by the author.

Disclaimer

This companion guide is provided for informational purposes only. While every effort has been made to ensure accuracy, the author, Dennis Pearson, and the publisher make no guarantees or warranties about the completeness or reliability of the content. Travel conditions and regulations may change, and it is the reader's responsibility to verify details with relevant authorities. The author is not liable for any errors, omissions, or outcomes resulting from the use of this guide. Readers should use their own judgment and seek professional advice where necessary.

TABLE OF CONTENTS

Chapter 1: Introduction to Luxor
- ❖ Welcome to Luxor
- ❖ My Personal Experience in Luxor
- ❖ Why Luxor? A Brief Overview
- ❖ What to Expect in 2025
- ❖ Health and Safety Tips
- ❖ Travel Insurance Recommendations

Chapter 2: Planning Your Trip
- ❖ When to Visit Luxor
- ❖ Travel Documentation and Visas
- ❖ Travel Tips for International Visitors
- ❖ Travel Essentials For Your Trip

Chapter 3: Getting There and Getting Around
- ❖ Airlines Serving Luxor
- ❖ Arrival and Airport Information
- ❖ Transportation from the Airport
- ❖ Public Transportation
- ❖ Car Rentals and Driving Tips
- ❖ Taxi and Ride-Sharing Services

Chapter 4: Accommodation and Dining in Luxor
- ❖ Overview of Lodging in Luxor
- ❖ Recommended Hotels
- ❖ Budget-Friendly Stays
- ❖ Luxury Accommodations
- ❖ Unique and Boutique Hotels
- ❖ Must-Try Dishes and Local Specialties
- ❖ Recommended Restaurants and Cafes
- ❖ Street Food and Food Markets

Chapter 5: Exploring Luxor Wonders
Must-Visit Attractions
- ❖ The Valley of the Kings
- ❖ Karnak Temple
- ❖ Luxor Temple
- ❖ The Temple of Hatshepsut
- ❖ The Colossi of Memnon
- ❖ The Temple of Medinet Habu
- ❖ Luxor Museum
- ❖ Hidden Gems and Off-the-Beaten-Path
- ❖ Lesser-Known Temples and Ruins
- ❖ Local Markets and Crafts
- ❖ Scenic Spots and Natural Wonders
- ❖ Unique Experiences and Activities

Chapter 6: Practical Information and Travel Tips

- ❖ Banks and Currency Exchange
- ❖ ATMs and Credit Card Usage
- ❖ Emergency Contacts and Services
- ❖ Local Laws and Regulations
- ❖ Health Services and Medical Facilities
- ❖ Safety and Security Advice
- ❖ Cultural Sensitivity Tips
- ❖ Essential Phrases in Arabic
- ❖ Navigating Common Challenges

Chapter 7 :Sample Itineraries and Useful Contacts

- ❖ 3-Day Adventure Itinerary
- ❖ 5-Day Cultural Exploration
- ❖ 7-Day Ultimate Luxor Experience
- ❖ Customizable Itinerary Tips
- ❖ Tourist Information Centers
- ❖ Local Guides and Tour Operators
- ❖ Itinerary Planner For Your Adventure

CHAPTER ONE

Introduction to Luxor

Luxor, which is situated far away in southern Egypt along the banks of the Nile River, is a monument to the majesty and mystique of ancient Egyptian civilization. Luxor, sometimes referred to as the "world's greatest open-air museum," is a city where mythology and history meet, providing a window into a past era that never fails to pique the interest of tourists and academics alike.

Luxor was formerly known as Thebes, and it served as Egypt's capital during the New Kingdom's heyday (1550–1070 BCE). The monuments, temples, and tombs of this ancient metropolis, which served as the political and religious center of Egypt, attest to its important place in the annals of one of the most powerful civilizations in history. The city's amazing collection of archaeological treasures, which includes some of the most famous and well-preserved sites from ancient Egypt, is a reflection of its rich heritage.

The Valley of the Kings and the Valley of the Queens, where pharaohs and nobles' tombs are embellished with elaborate hieroglyphs and breathtaking frescoes, are two of Luxor's most well-known sites. One of the biggest religious buildings ever constructed, the adjacent Karnak Temple Complex, is a striking example of the architectural and artistic prowess of the ancient Egyptians. Another example of the city's former magnificence is the Luxor Temple, which is not far from Karnak and features massive columns and statues.

Luxor's appeal extends beyond its historical sites. The city's vibrant markets, bustling with local life, provide an opportunity to experience traditional Egyptian culture and cuisine. Visitors can wander through lively souks, sample local delicacies, and purchase handcrafted souvenirs. The city's modern amenities and hospitality ensure a comfortable stay, blending seamlessly with its ancient charm.

The natural beauty of Luxor is equally captivating. The Nile River, which flows gracefully through the city, offers opportunities for serene boat rides and breathtaking views. The surrounding landscape, dotted with lush palm groves and arid desert expanses, enhances the city's allure, making it a photographer's paradise.

Luxor's strategic location as a hub of ancient Egyptian civilization makes it a vital destination for those interested in exploring Egypt's rich historical tapestry. As you prepare for your journey, you will find that Luxor not only provides a profound historical experience but also offers a welcoming atmosphere that embraces the timeless essence of its past.

In this guide, we aim to equip you with all the information you need to make the most of your visit to Luxor. From navigating its remarkable sites to understanding its cultural nuances, this comprehensive companion will help you embark on a memorable and enriching adventure in one of the world's most extraordinary cities.

My Personal Experience in Luxor

I left my hotel and entered an almost otherworldly world as the first light of dawn painted the sky over Luxor. Bathed in the golden light of the early morning sun, the ancient city unfurled before me like a vast, dynamic work of history and mystery.

I started my journey by going to the Valley of the Kings, a location that had long captivated my interest. The air grew colder and the shadows grew deeper as I made my way down into the tombs. The walls were covered in elaborate hieroglyphics and colorful frescoes that depicted gods, pharaohs, and the afterlife. Every tomb was an exquisite work of ancient art, and I could practically hear the ghosts of the past as I strolled through these hallowed chambers. I experienced a thrill of excitement as I stood in front of Tutankhamun's tomb, anticipating an encounter with the fabled boy king.

After the awe-inspiring tombs, I made my way to the Karnak Temple Complex. As I approached, the sheer scale of the site took my breath away. The towering columns of the Great Hypostyle Hall, adorned with elaborate carvings, seemed to reach up into the heavens. I marveled at the grandeur of the temple, imagining the priests and worshippers who once filled this sacred space with rituals and ceremonies. The sun was setting, casting a warm glow over the ancient stones, and the experience was nothing short of magical.

One evening, I ventured into Luxor's bustling market, a vibrant tapestry of sights and sounds. The aroma of freshly baked bread and spicy falafel wafted through the air, mingling with the scents of incense and spices. I found myself drawn to a small stall where an elderly vendor was selling intricately woven scarves. We exchanged smiles and stories, and I couldn't resist purchasing one of his beautiful creations as a keepsake.

My exploration took a serene turn as I boarded a felucca, a traditional wooden sailboat, for a sunset cruise on the Nile River. As the boat glided along the river's calm waters, the lush green banks and distant temples created a picturesque landscape. The sky transformed into a canvas of oranges and pinks, reflecting in the tranquil waters below. It was a moment of peaceful reflection, a perfect ending to a day filled with wonder.

One of the most memorable experiences of my trip was a visit to the Temple of Hatshepsut, perched majestically against the backdrop of rocky cliffs. As I climbed the terraces and gazed out over the valley below, I felt a profound connection to the powerful female pharaoh who had commissioned this architectural marvel. The temple's grandeur and the surrounding landscape created a sense of timelessness, a reminder of the enduring legacy of ancient Egypt.

I took one last glance at the city that had captured my heart as I boarded my flight home. Luxor had left its mark on me with its vibrant life and ancient wonders, and I knew I would always be surrounded by its magic.

Why Luxor? A Brief Overview

Luxor, often hailed as the "world's greatest open-air museum," offers an unparalleled journey through one of the most fascinating chapters of ancient Egyptian history. Located on the east bank of the Nile River, Luxor was once known as Thebes, the grand capital of the New Kingdom period (1550-1070 BCE). The city is a living testament to the might and mystery of ancient Egypt, home to some of the most remarkable and well-preserved archaeological treasures ever discovered.

The allure of Luxor lies in its rich tapestry of history, culture, and mythology. It boasts an array of iconic sites, including the Valley of the Kings, where the tombs of pharaohs like Tutankhamun and Ramses VI are adorned with stunning frescoes and inscriptions. The Karnak Temple Complex, a sprawling collection of temples and sanctuaries, stands as a monumental achievement in ancient architecture. Meanwhile, the Luxor Temple, with its towering columns and grand statues, serves as a striking symbol of the city's historical significance.

Beyond its historical sites, Luxor offers a vibrant and dynamic experience. The city's markets bustle with local life, providing an opportunity to engage with Egyptian culture through its food, crafts, and traditions. The serene Nile River, which flows through the city, offers picturesque views and tranquil boat rides, adding a touch of natural beauty to the historical splendor.

What to Expect in 2025

As you plan your visit to Luxor in 2024-2025, you can expect a blend of enduring historical grandeur and modern amenities. The city remains a top destination for history enthusiasts, with ongoing archaeological discoveries and conservation efforts enhancing the visitor experience. New technologies and improved infrastructure aim to make your journey more enjoyable, with updated visitor centers, enhanced digital guides, and more accessible information about the city's many attractions.

Luxor is continuously evolving, with new hotels, restaurants, and cultural experiences emerging to cater to a diverse range of travelers. Expect improved connectivity and services, making it easier to navigate the city and explore its treasures. Advances in conservation and presentation will offer fresh perspectives on ancient sites, ensuring that each visit provides a unique and enriching experience.

Health and Safety Tips

Traveling to Luxor, like any international destination, requires some preparation to ensure a safe and enjoyable trip. Here are some essential health and safety tips:

Stay Hydrated and Protect Against the Sun: Luxor's climate can be extremely hot, especially during the summer months. Drink plenty of bottled water, use sunscreen, and wear a hat and sunglasses to protect yourself from the sun.

Be Cautious with Food and Water: To avoid foodborne illnesses, eat at reputable restaurants and avoid consuming raw or undercooked foods. Stick to bottled or purified water, and ensure that the seal on the bottle is intact before opening.

Use Health Insurance Wisely: Make sure you have comprehensive travel health insurance that covers medical emergencies, including evacuation if necessary. Check with your insurance provider to understand the extent of your coverage in Egypt.

Stay Informed About Local Health Risks: Before traveling, consult travel health advisories for any specific vaccinations or health precautions recommended for

Egypt. It's also a good idea to carry a basic first aid kit with essentials like band-aids, pain relievers, and any personal medications.

Follow Local Guidelines: Adhere to local laws and regulations, and be mindful of cultural norms. Respect local customs, especially when visiting religious sites, and follow any safety advisories issued by local authorities.

Travel Insurance Recommendations

Travel insurance is a vital aspect of planning a trip to Luxor, as it provides financial protection and peace of mind. Here's what to consider when selecting travel insurance:

Medical Coverage: Ensure your policy offers comprehensive medical coverage, including emergency medical treatment and evacuation. This is crucial for addressing any unforeseen health issues that may arise during your trip.

Trip Cancellation and Interruption: Look for insurance that covers trip cancellations, interruptions, or delays due to unforeseen circumstances, such as illness or natural disasters. This can help recover non-refundable expenses if your travel plans are disrupted.

Lost or Stolen Belongings: Choose a policy that covers lost, stolen, or damaged luggage and personal belongings. This can be particularly useful if you're carrying valuable items or electronics.

Emergency Assistance: Select a policy that provides access to 24/7 emergency assistance services. This can be invaluable in coordinating medical care, replacing lost documents, or navigating unexpected situations.

Pre-Existing Conditions: If you have any pre-existing medical conditions, check that your insurance policy covers these conditions or provides an option for additional coverage.

CHAPTER TWO

Planning Your Trip

When to Visit Luxor

Luxor, with its rich tapestry of ancient history and vibrant local culture, is a destination that offers something special year-round. However, the best time to visit largely depends on your preferences for weather and crowd levels.

Optimal Time for Visiting

The most favorable time to visit Luxor is during the cooler months from October to April. During this period, temperatures are milder and more comfortable, ranging from 15°C to 25°C (59°F to 77°F). This is ideal for exploring Luxor's extensive archaeological sites and enjoying outdoor activities without the intense heat of the summer months.

Seasonal Considerations

Winter (December to February): This is peak tourist season in Luxor due to the pleasant temperatures and clear skies. It's an excellent time for sightseeing and participating in outdoor activities, but it can also be quite busy, so booking accommodations and tours in advance is advisable.

Spring (March to May): Spring is another great time to visit Luxor. The weather is warm but not excessively hot, and the crowds are generally smaller compared to the winter season. This period is ideal for those seeking a balance between good weather and fewer tourists.

Summer (June to August): Summer in Luxor can be extremely hot, with temperatures often exceeding 40°C (104°F). While the heat may be intense, this is also the least crowded time, and you might find better deals on accommodations. If you choose to visit during this time, plan to explore early in the morning or later in the evening to avoid the midday heat.

Autumn (September to November): Autumn offers a transition from the intense summer heat to more comfortable temperatures. It's a good time to visit if you want to avoid the peak winter crowds while still enjoying pleasant weather.

Travel Documentation and Visas

To visit Luxor, travelers need to ensure they have the appropriate documentation and visas. The requirements can vary depending on your nationality, but here is a general overview of what is needed:

Visa Requirements
Tourist Visa: Most travelers require a tourist visa to enter Egypt. This visa can usually be obtained either upon arrival at Egyptian airports or in advance from an Egyptian consulate or embassy. It is advisable to check the specific requirements based on your nationality.

E-Visa: Egypt offers an e-visa system that allows travelers to apply for a visa online before their trip. The e-visa process is straightforward and can be completed through the official Egyptian government website. This option is convenient and often faster than obtaining a visa on arrival.

Visa on Arrival: For many nationalities, a tourist visa can be obtained upon arrival at Egyptian airports. This visa typically allows for a stay of up to 30 days. Be prepared to show proof of onward travel and sufficient funds for your stay.

❖ Travel Documentation

Passport: Ensure your passport is valid for at least six months beyond your planned departure date from Egypt. It should also have at least one blank page for the visa.

Travel Insurance: While not a visa requirement, having travel insurance is highly recommended. It provides coverage for medical emergencies, trip cancellations, and other unexpected events.

Travel Itinerary: It's a good idea to have a copy of your travel itinerary, including accommodation details and return flight information, as you may be asked for this information upon entry.

Vaccinations and Health Precautions: Depending on your country of origin, certain vaccinations may be recommended or required. It is prudent to check with your healthcare provider or a travel clinic before your trip.

Travel Tips for International Visitors

Traveling to Luxor from abroad involves some essential preparations and considerations to ensure a smooth and enjoyable experience. Here are some valuable travel tips for international visitors:

1. Understand Local Customs and Etiquette: Egypt has its own unique cultural norms and traditions. Familiarize yourself with local customs, such as dress codes for religious sites and social interactions. Modest clothing is recommended, especially when visiting temples and mosques. Learning a few basic Arabic phrases can also be helpful and appreciated by locals.

2. Currency and Payments: The local currency in Egypt is the Egyptian Pound (EGP). While credit and debit cards are accepted in many hotels and restaurants, it's advisable to carry some cash for small purchases and transactions in markets or rural areas. Currency exchange services are available at airports, banks, and exchange bureaus.

3. Safety Precautions: Luxor is generally safe for tourists, but it's always wise to exercise common sense. Avoid displaying valuable items and be cautious in crowded places. Follow local advice and be aware of your surroundings. Emergency services can be reached by dialing 122 for police, 123 for ambulance, and 180 for fire.

4. Local Transportation: Public transportation in Luxor includes taxis, microbuses, and feluccas (traditional boats). Agree on taxi fares before starting your journey or use ride-hailing apps if available. For a more authentic experience, consider hiring a local guide or joining organized tours to navigate the city and its historical sites.

5. Health Precautions: Drink bottled or purified water to avoid waterborne illnesses. Be cautious with street food and choose reputable vendors to reduce the risk of food-related issues. It's a good idea to carry hand sanitizer and basic first-aid supplies.

6. Respect for Historical Sites: When visiting archaeological sites, follow guidelines to help preserve these valuable treasures. Avoid touching or leaning on ancient structures, and refrain from taking photos where prohibited. Respect the rules set by site officials to ensure a positive experience for everyone.

7. Stay Hydrated and Sun Safe: Luxor's climate can be extremely hot, especially in the summer months. Drink plenty of water, wear sunscreen, a hat, and sunglasses to protect yourself from the sun. Take breaks in shaded areas and avoid prolonged exposure during peak heat hours.

8. Communication and Connectivity: International travelers can use their mobile phones in Egypt, but it's worth checking with your service provider about roaming charges. Alternatively, you can purchase a local SIM card for affordable data and calling options.

9. Emergency Contacts: Keep a list of important contacts, including your embassy or consulate, local emergency services, and your accommodation. Having this information readily available can be useful in case of unexpected situations.

Travel Essentials for Your Trip

When preparing for your trip to Luxor, it's important to pack and organize essential items to ensure a comfortable and hassle-free experience. Here's a checklist of travel essentials:

1. Passport and Visa: Ensure your passport is valid for at least six months beyond your intended stay. Carry your visa or e-visa approval if applicable.

2. Travel Insurance: Bring a copy of your travel insurance policy and emergency contact numbers. Ensure it covers medical emergencies, trip cancellations, and other travel-related issues.

3. Currency and Payment Methods: Pack some Egyptian Pounds for cash transactions. Also, carry credit or debit cards for payments where accepted. Keep both cash and cards in a secure place.

4. Clothing: Pack lightweight, breathable clothing suitable for hot weather. Include modest attire for visits to religious sites, such as long skirts or trousers and tops with sleeves. Bring a light jacket or sweater for cooler evenings and air-conditioned environments.

5. Footwear: Comfortable walking shoes are essential for exploring Luxor's historical sites. Consider packing sandals for casual wear and sturdier shoes for more extensive walking or trekking.

6. Health and Hygiene Supplies: Include any personal medications, a basic first-aid kit, sunscreen, insect repellent, hand sanitizer, and any special health items you may need.

7. Electronics and Gadgets: Bring a camera or smartphone for capturing memories, along with chargers and any necessary adapters for Egyptian power outlets (type C and type F).

8. Travel Guides and Maps: Although you'll have access to information digitally, having a physical travel guide or map can be useful for navigating Luxor and its attractions.

9. Personal Comfort Items: Pack items for personal comfort, such as a reusable water bottle, a hat for sun protection, and a travel pillow if you plan on long journeys or flights.

10. Important Documents: Keep copies of important documents such as your itinerary, accommodation details, and emergency contacts in a separate location from the originals.

By following these tips and preparing these essentials, you'll be well-equipped for a memorable and enjoyable visit to Luxor.

CHAPTER THREE

Getting There and Getting Around

Airlines Serving Luxor

Luxor is well-connected to several major international and regional destinations through its primary airport, Luxor International Airport (LXR). Various airlines provide services to and from this key Egyptian gateway, catering to travelers from around the globe. Below is a broad overview of airlines that frequently serve Luxor, including their contact information and addresses.

1. EgyptAir
    - **Address: EgyptAir Building, 5 El Moussadak Street, Dokki, Cairo, Egypt**
    - **Contact Information: +20 2 261 82000**
    - **Website: egyptair.com**

As Egypt's flagship carrier, EgyptAir offers direct flights to Luxor from Cairo, as well as connections from various international cities.

2. Turkish Airlines
    - **Address: Turkish Airlines Office, Tahrir Square, Cairo, Egypt**
    - **Contact Information: +20 2 257 50980**

- Website: turkishairlines.com

Turkish Airlines provides connections between Luxor and Istanbul, facilitating access to various international destinations.

3. Lufthansa
- **Address: Lufthansa Office, 9 Al-Azhar Street, Cairo, Egypt**
- **Contact Information: +20 2 2390 1191**
- **Website: lufthansa.com**

Lufthansa offers flights to Luxor via connections through its European hubs, including Frankfurt and Munich.

4. Air France
- **Address: Air France Office, 12 El-Galaa Street, Cairo, Egypt**
- **Contact Information: +20 2 3330 4500**
- **Website: airfrance.com**

Air France connects Luxor with Paris and other French cities, providing additional options for travelers coming from Europe.

5. Swiss International Air Lines
- **Address: Swiss International Air Lines Office, 9th Floor, City Stars, Cairo, Egypt**
- **Contact Information: +20 2 2670 3234**
- **Website: swiss.com**

Swiss International Air Lines offers flights to Luxor from its main Swiss hubs, including Zurich.

Arrival and Airport Information

Luxor International Airport (LXR) is the primary airport serving the city of Luxor. Here's a comprehensive overview of the airport's facilities and services:

- **Address: Luxor International Airport, Luxor, Egypt**
- **Contact Information: +20 95 238 1363**
- **Website: luxor-airport.com**

Luxor International Airport is a modern facility equipped with amenities to make your arrival as smooth as possible. It features a range of services including baggage claim, customs and immigration, currency exchange, and car rental counters. The airport also provides facilities such as lounges, dining options, and retail shops for convenience and comfort.

Transportation from the Airport

Upon arrival at Luxor International Airport, you have several options for transportation to reach your accommodation or begin exploring the city:

1. Taxis: Taxis are readily available outside the arrivals area. It's advisable to use authorized taxis and agree on the fare before starting your journey. Some taxis might not have meters, so negotiating the price in advance is recommended.

2. Airport Shuttle Services: Many hotels in Luxor offer airport shuttle services for their guests. Check with your accommodation in advance to arrange for a shuttle pickup. This can be a convenient option, especially if you have a lot of luggage.

3. Car Rentals: If you prefer to drive yourself, several car rental agencies operate at Luxor International Airport. Major international and local car rental companies provide services, allowing you to explore Luxor and its surroundings at your own pace.

4. Private Transfers: Private transfer services can be booked in advance through travel agencies or online platforms. These services offer the convenience of a pre-arranged vehicle and driver, ensuring a hassle-free transfer from the airport to your destination.

5. Local Buses: While less common, local buses do operate in and out of the airport. However, they may not be the most convenient option for travelers with significant luggage or those unfamiliar with the local routes.

6. Ride-Sharing Services: If available, ride-sharing apps may offer a convenient and potentially cost-effective way to get from the airport to your accommodation. Be sure to check the local regulations and availability of such services before your trip.

Each of these transportation options provides different levels of comfort and convenience, so choose the one that best fits your needs and preferences.

Public Transportation in Luxor

Luxor offers various public transportation options to help visitors navigate the city and its surroundings. Here is an overview of the primary public transportation methods available:

1. Local Buses

Service Overview: Local buses in Luxor operate routes within the city and to nearby areas. They are an affordable option for getting around but may be less comfortable and less reliable compared to other forms of transportation.

2. Microbuses

Service Overview: Microbuses are a common and economical form of transportation in Luxor, often used by locals for short to medium distances. They usually have set routes and are a practical option for reaching various parts of the city.

Car Rentals and Driving Tips

Renting a car in Luxor provides the flexibility to explore the city and the surrounding region at your own pace. Below is a list of car rental companies in Luxor, along with their contact details and addresses:

1. Hertz
   - **Address: Luxor Airport, Luxor, Egypt**
   - **Contact Information: +20 95 238 1166**
   - **Website: hertz.com**

Hertz offers a range of rental vehicles at Luxor International Airport, providing convenient access for travelers arriving by air.

2. Avis
   - **Address: Luxor International Airport, Luxor, Egypt**
   - **Contact Information: +20 95 238 0628**
   - **Website: avis.com**

Avis provides car rental services at the airport, offering options for both short-term and long-term rentals.

3. Budget

- Address: Luxor International Airport, Luxor, Egypt
- Contact Information: +20 95 238 0628
- Website: budget.com

Budget is known for its competitive rates and range of vehicles available for rent at Luxor International Airport.

4. Sixt

- Address: Luxor International Airport, Luxor, Egypt
- Contact Information: +20 95 238 1363
- Website: sixt.com

Sixt offers a variety of rental options at the airport, including luxury and standard vehicles.

Driving Tips in Luxor

Road Conditions: Roads in Luxor are generally in good condition, but driving can be chaotic compared to Western standards. Be prepared for local driving habits and frequent use of horns.

Traffic Rules: Adhere to local traffic laws and regulations. Traffic lights and road signs are present but may not always be followed by local drivers.
Parking: Parking can be challenging in busy areas. Look for designated parking areas and be cautious of restricted zones.
Navigation: GPS and maps can be helpful, but local knowledge of routes and landmarks is beneficial. Consider using a GPS navigation system or app.
Insurance: Ensure that your rental car insurance covers any potential accidents or damage.

Taxi and Ride-Sharing Services

1. Taxis
Service Overview: Taxis are widely available in Luxor and are a convenient way to travel within the city. It is advisable to use reputable taxi services or arrange taxis through your hotel to ensure a fair fare.

2. Ride-Sharing Services
Uber
Service Overview: Uber operates in Luxor, providing an easy-to-use app for booking rides with set fares. It's a reliable option for getting around the city with the convenience of cashless payment.

- Website: uber.com

Careem

Service Overview: Careem is another popular ride-sharing app in Egypt, offering similar services to Uber. It allows users to book rides, track their drivers, and pay via the app.

Website: careem.com
Using Taxis and Ride-Sharing Services

- **Taxi Tips:** Always confirm the fare before starting your journey, as not all taxis use meters. Ensure the driver is authorized and that the vehicle is in good condition.
- **Ride-Sharing Tips:** Use the app to check driver details and fare estimates. Communicate clearly with your driver and ensure they follow the route as shown in the app.

CHAPTER FOUR

Accommodation and Dining in Luxor

Overview of Lodging in Luxor

Luxor offers a range of lodging options to suit different preferences and budgets. From luxurious hotels with stunning Nile views to charming boutique accommodations and budget-friendly choices, visitors can find a variety of options that cater to their needs. Here's a broad overview of lodging options in Luxor:

1. Luxury Hotels
Luxor is home to several high-end hotels that offer luxurious amenities, exceptional service, and breathtaking views of the Nile or ancient monuments. These hotels often feature spacious rooms, fine dining restaurants, swimming pools, and spa facilities, providing a premium experience for travelers.

2. Mid-Range Hotels
For those seeking comfort without the extravagance, mid-range hotels in Luxor provide a balance of quality

and affordability. These hotels typically offer well-appointed rooms, convenient services, and a good location close to major attractions.

3. Budget Accommodations
Luxor also caters to budget-conscious travelers with a variety of affordable lodging options. These include guesthouses, hostels, and budget hotels that provide basic amenities and a comfortable stay for those looking to save on accommodation costs.

4. Boutique Hotels
Boutique hotels in Luxor offer a more personalized and unique experience. Often smaller in size, these hotels focus on individual style and character, providing guests with a distinctive atmosphere and a closer connection to local culture.

Recommended Hotels

Here are some of the top recommended hotels in Luxor, each offering its own unique advantages and features:

1. Sofitel Winter Palace Luxor
   - **Address: Corniche El Nile, Luxor, Egypt**
   - **Contact Information: +20 95 238 0230**
   - **Website: sofitel.com**

A historic luxury hotel overlooking the Nile River, Sofitel Winter Palace Luxor is renowned for its elegant architecture, opulent interiors, and exceptional service. The hotel features beautiful gardens, a grand dining room, and a luxurious spa, making it a top choice for travelers seeking a high-end experience.

2. Hilton Luxor Resort & Spa
   - **Address: P.O. Box 13, New Karnak, Luxor, Egypt**
   - **Contact Information: +20 95 238 1430**
   - **Website: hilton.com**

Located along the Nile, Hilton Luxor Resort & Spa offers stunning river views, a spacious pool area, and modern amenities. The resort provides a relaxing atmosphere with a full-service spa, multiple dining options, and easy access to Luxor's major attractions.

3. Steigenberger Nile Palace Luxor
- Address: Khaled Ibn El Walid Street, Luxor, Egypt
- Contact Information: +20 95 238 1130
- Website: steigenberger.com

Steigenberger Nile Palace combines comfort and luxury with panoramic views of the Nile. The hotel features elegantly decorated rooms, a variety of dining options, a large pool, and a well-equipped fitness center.

4. Al Moudira Hotel
- Address: West Bank, Luxor, Egypt
- Contact Information: +20 95 238 0353
- Website: almoudira.com

Situated on the West Bank of Luxor, Al Moudira Hotel offers a unique blend of traditional Egyptian architecture and modern comfort. The boutique hotel is known for its personalized service, lush gardens, and tranquil atmosphere.

5. Nefertiti Hotel
- Address: 10 El Moudira Street, Luxor, Egypt
- Contact Information: +20 95 238 2741
- Website: nefertitihotel.com

Nefertiti Hotel is a mid-range option that provides a comfortable stay with views of the Nile and proximity to Luxor's main attractions. The hotel offers a friendly atmosphere, clean rooms, and a rooftop restaurant with stunning views.

6. El Luxor Hotel
- **Address: 5 El Moudira Street, Luxor, Egypt**
- **Contact Information: +20 95 238 0646**
- **Website: luxorhotel.com**

El Luxor Hotel is a budget-friendly choice with simple yet comfortable accommodations. It is conveniently located near the city center, making it a practical option for travelers looking to explore Luxor without spending a fortune.

7. Lotus Hotel
- **Address: 16 Corniche El Nile, Luxor, Egypt**
- **Contact Information: +20 95 238 0867**
- **Website: lotushotel.com**

Lotus Hotel offers affordable accommodations with a focus on comfort and convenience. The hotel features a central location, making it easy to access local attractions and amenities.

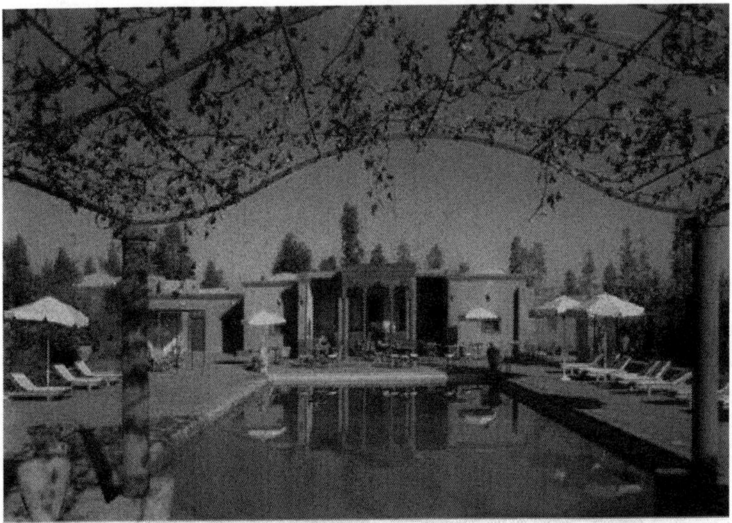

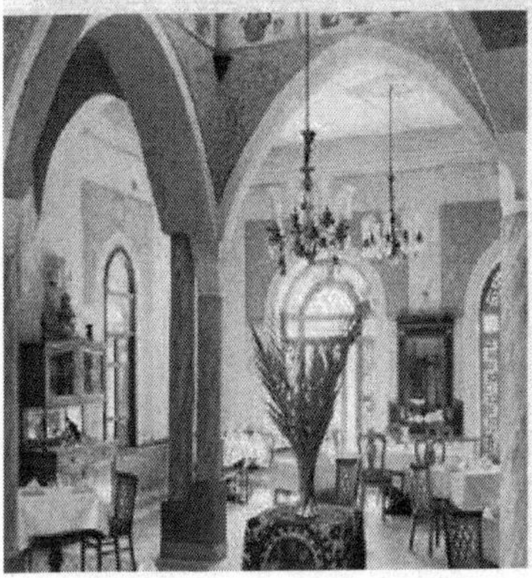

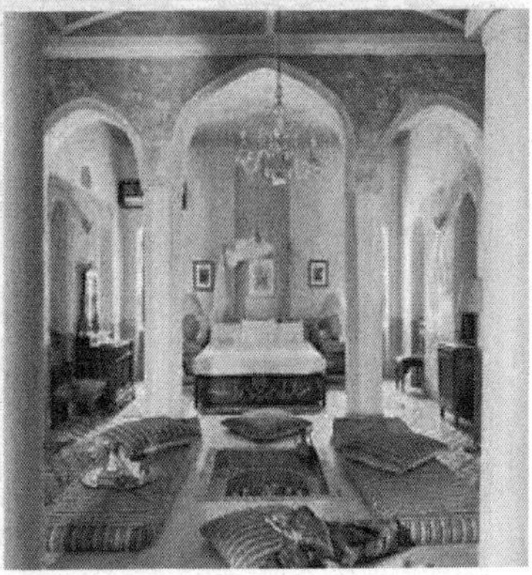

Must-Try Dishes and Local Specialties

Luxor boasts a rich culinary heritage with a variety of delicious dishes and local specialties. When visiting, be sure to try these iconic Egyptian foods:

1. Koshari
Description: A hearty and popular Egyptian dish made from rice, lentils, and macaroni, topped with a spicy tomato sauce, chickpeas, and crispy fried onions. It's often served with a side of garlic vinegar and hot sauce.
Where to Try: Local restaurants and street food vendors throughout Luxor.

2. Ful Medames
Description: A traditional breakfast dish consisting of fava beans stewed with olive oil, garlic, and lemon juice. It's typically served with pita bread and garnished with tomatoes, cucumbers, and onions.
Where to Try: Popular at breakfast spots and local eateries.

3. Taameya (Egyptian Falafel)
Description: Made from mashed fava beans instead of chickpeas, taameya is a spiced and deep-fried patty, often served in pita bread with salad and tahini sauce.

Where to Try: Street food vendors and casual dining spots.

4. Mahshi
Description: Vegetables such as zucchini, bell peppers, and grape leaves stuffed with a mixture of rice, herbs, and spices. The dish is cooked in a tomato-based sauce.
Where to Try: Traditional restaurants offering Egyptian home-style cooking.

5. Shawarma
Description: A popular Middle Eastern dish of marinated meat (usually chicken or beef) that is roasted on a vertical rotisserie and served in a wrap with vegetables and sauces.
Where to Try: Fast food joints and street vendors.

6. Egyptian Mezze
Description: A variety of small dishes served as appetizers, including hummus, baba ganoush (eggplant dip), and tabbouleh (herb salad).
Where to Try: Restaurants specializing in Middle Eastern cuisine.

7. Basbousa
Description: A sweet semolina cake soaked in syrup and often topped with coconut or almonds. It's a popular Egyptian dessert.
Where to Try: Bakeries and dessert shops.

Recommended Restaurants and Cafes

Luxor offers a diverse range of dining options, from upscale restaurants to charming cafes. Here are some top recommendations:

1. **1886 Restaurant**
   - **Address:** Sofitel Winter Palace Luxor, Corniche El Nile, Luxor, Egypt
   - **Contact Information:** +20 95 238 0230
   - **Website:** sofitel.com

Located in the historic Sofitel Winter Palace, 1886 Restaurant offers fine dining with an elegant atmosphere. The menu features international and Egyptian cuisine prepared with high-quality ingredients.

2. **The Lantern Room**
   - **Address:** 4 El Moudira Street, Luxor, Egypt
   - **Contact Information:** +20 95 238 1676
   - **Website:** thelanternroom.com

This cozy restaurant is known for its delicious Egyptian and Mediterranean dishes, as well as its warm and welcoming ambiance.

3. **Sunflower Restaurant**
   - Address: 7 Corniche El Nile, Luxor, Egypt

- Contact Information: +20 95 238 2067
- Website: sunflowerluxor.com

A favorite among locals and tourists alike, Sunflower Restaurant offers a range of traditional Egyptian dishes and a friendly atmosphere.

4. El-Fayoum Restaurant
- Address: 14 El Moudira Street, Luxor, Egypt
- Contact Information: +20 95 238 0742
- Website: elfayoum.com

Known for its authentic Egyptian cuisine, El-Fayoum Restaurant provides a traditional dining experience with a variety of local specialties.

5. Afrodit Restaurant
- **Address: 8 Khaled Ibn El Walid Street, Luxor, Egypt**
- **Contact Information: +20 95 238 1910**
- Website: afroditluxor.com

Afrodit Restaurant offers a mix of Egyptian and international dishes, along with a comfortable setting and attentive service.

Street Food and Food Markets

Experiencing local street food and markets is a great way to immerse yourself in Egyptian culture and cuisine. Here are some popular spots to explore:

1. **Luxor Street Food Market**
Location: Various locations throughout Luxor, including near the central bus station and along the Corniche.
Overview: This bustling market features a variety of street food vendors offering local specialties such as koshari, taameya, and freshly squeezed juices. It's a lively place to sample affordable and authentic Egyptian street food.

2. **Karnak Village Market**
Location: Near Karnak Temple, Luxor, Egypt
Overview: The Karnak Village Market is a vibrant spot where you can find street food, local produce, and traditional Egyptian snacks. It's a great place to taste local delicacies and experience the local market atmosphere.

3. **Luxor Souq (Market)**
Location: Near Luxor Temple, Luxor, Egypt

Overview: This traditional market offers a range of goods, including spices, herbs, and street food. Vendors sell everything from freshly prepared falafel and kebabs to sweet treats like basbousa and kunafa.

4. El-Hussein Street Food
Location: El-Hussein Street, Luxor, Egypt
Overview: A popular area for street food lovers, El-Hussein Street offers a variety of quick and tasty Egyptian eats. It's a great place to try traditional dishes in a casual setting.

CHAPTER FIVE
Exploring Luxor Wonders

Must-Visit Attractions in Luxor

Luxor, often referred to as the world's greatest open-air museum, is home to a wealth of ancient Egyptian monuments and temples. Here's a detailed guide to some of the city's most iconic attractions:

The Valley of the Kings

The Valley of the Kings is one of Egypt's most significant archaeological sites, serving as the burial place for many of the pharaohs of the New Kingdom, including Tutankhamun, Ramses the Great, and Seti I. The valley contains over 60 tombs, decorated with elaborate murals and inscriptions that provide insight into the beliefs and funerary practices of ancient Egypt.

How to Get There:
The Valley of the Kings is located on the West Bank of the Nile River, approximately 5 kilometers (3 miles) from Luxor's city center. It is accessible by taxi or tour bus. Many local tour operators offer guided tours that include transportation to and from the site.

Address: Valley of the Kings, Luxor West Bank, Luxor, Egypt

Hours of Operation:
Typically open from 6:00 AM to 5:00 PM. Hours may vary, and it's advisable to check in advance.

Admission:
Tickets can be purchased at the site. Entrance fees vary based on the tombs you wish to visit. The standard ticket includes access to three tombs, with additional fees for special tombs.

Karnak Temple

Karnak Temple is one of the largest and most impressive religious complexes in Egypt. It was primarily dedicated to the god Amun-Ra and features a vast array of temples, chapels, pylons, and obelisks. The Great Hypostyle Hall, with its 134 massive columns, is a highlight, as is the Sacred Lake.

How to Get There: Karnak Temple is located about 2.5 kilometers (1.5 miles) north of Luxor Temple on the East Bank of the Nile. It can be reached by taxi, bicycle, or on foot from central Luxor. Many tour operators also include Karnak Temple in their guided tours.

Address: Karnak Temple, Karnak, Luxor, Egypt

Hours of Operation: Generally open from 6:00 AM to 5:30 PM, with extended hours during peak tourist seasons.

Admission: Tickets can be purchased at the site. There are also options for multi-site tickets that include other temples and tombs in Luxor.

Luxor Temple

Luxor Temple, located in the heart of Luxor on the East Bank, was originally constructed by Amenhotep III and later modified by Ramses II. The temple is known for its large entrance pylon, the Avenue of Sphinxes, and the beautifully preserved colonnade. It served as a key religious center and was the site of the Opet Festival, which celebrated the divine marriage of Amun-Ra and the goddess Mut.

How to Get There: Luxor Temple is centrally located in Luxor, making it easily accessible by walking from many central hotels. It is also reachable by taxi or bicycle. Visitors can also join guided tours that include Luxor Temple as part of the itinerary.

Address: Luxor Temple, Luxor, Egypt

Hours of Operation: Typically open from 6:00 AM to 9:00 PM. Hours may vary, so it's advisable to check in advance.

Admission: Tickets can be purchased at the entrance. There are options for single-site tickets or multi-site passes.

The Temple of Hatshepsut

The Temple of Hatshepsut, also known as Deir el-Bahari, is a mortuary temple dedicated to Queen Hatshepsut, one of Egypt's most remarkable female pharaohs. The temple is renowned for its impressive terraced structure, carved into the cliffs of the Theban mountains. It features stunning colonnades, statues, and reliefs depicting Hatshepsut's divine birth, her expedition to Punt, and various religious rituals.

How to Get There: The Temple of Hatshepsut is located on the West Bank of the Nile River, approximately 8 kilometers (5 miles) from Luxor's city center. It is easily accessible by taxi, tour bus, or as part of a guided tour that includes other West Bank sites.

Address: Temple of Hatshepsut, Deir el-Bahari, West Bank, Luxor, Egypt

Hours of Operation: Typically open from 6:00 AM to 5:00 PM. Hours may vary depending on the season, so it is advisable to check in advance.

Admission: Tickets can be purchased at the site. It's possible to buy combined tickets for multiple sites on the West Bank.

The Colossi of Memnon

The Colossi of Memnon are two massive statues of Pharaoh Amenhotep III, standing at around 18 meters (60 feet) tall. These colossal figures once flanked the entrance to Amenhotep III's mortuary temple, which has since been largely destroyed. The statues are famous for their impressive size and for the acoustic phenomenon known as the "vocal Memnon," where the statues were said to produce mysterious sounds at dawn during the Roman period.

How to Get There: The Colossi of Memnon are located on the West Bank of the Nile River, near the entrance to the Valley of the Kings and the Temple of Hatshepsut. They can be visited by taxi or as part of a West Bank tour.

Address: Colossi of Memnon, West Bank, Luxor, Egypt

Hours of Operation: Accessible at all times, as the statues are located in an open area. However, visits are generally made during daylight hours.

Admission: There is no separate admission fee for the Colossi of Memnon; it is typically included in the ticket for other West Bank sites.

The Temple of Medinet Habu

The Temple of Medinet Habu is one of the best-preserved temples on the West Bank and was built by Ramses III. The temple complex is known for its impressive defensive walls, massive pylon entrance, and extensive reliefs depicting Ramses III's military campaigns and rituals. It served as both a religious center and a fortification, reflecting its dual role in ancient Egyptian society.

How to Get There: The Temple of Medinet Habu is located on the West Bank of the Nile River, approximately 10 kilometers (6 miles) from Luxor. It can be reached by taxi or as part of a guided tour of West Bank sites.

Address: Temple of Medinet Habu, West Bank, Luxor, Egypt

Hours of Operation: Typically open from 6:00 AM to 5:00 PM. Check ahead for any seasonal changes in operating hours.

Admission: Tickets are available at the site, with options for combined tickets for multiple West Bank attractions.

Luxor Museum

The Luxor Museum is a modern museum showcasing a rich collection of artifacts from the Theban necropolis and surrounding areas. Highlights include statues, mummies, and relics from the tombs of the Valley of the Kings, as well as exhibits on ancient Egyptian art and daily life. The museum provides a comprehensive overview of Luxor's archaeological heritage.

How to Get There: The Luxor Museum is located on the East Bank of the Nile River, near the city center and Luxor Temple. It is easily accessible by walking, taxi, or as part of a broader tour of Luxor's attractions.
Address: Luxor Museum, Khaled Ibn El Walid Street, Luxor, Egypt

- Contact Information:
- Phone: +20 95 237 4148
- Website: luxormuseum.com (

Hours of Operation: Typically open from 9:00 AM to 9:00 PM, with extended hours during peak tourist seasons. It is advisable to confirm current hours before visiting.

Admission: Tickets can be purchased at the entrance. The museum often offers combined tickets with other cultural sites in Luxor.

Hidden Gems and Off-the-Beaten-Path Attractions in Luxor

Luxor is well-known for its major archaeological sites, but it also offers a range of lesser-known attractions and hidden gems that provide a unique and intimate experience of Egypt's ancient and contemporary culture. Here are some off-the-beaten-path places to explore:

Lesser-Known Temples and Ruins

1. Temple of Seti I at Qurna
The Temple of Seti I, located in the village of Qurna on the West Bank, is a lesser-visited site compared to its more famous neighbors. The temple is dedicated to the god Amun-Ra and features well-preserved reliefs depicting the king's military campaigns and religious rituals. The temple's location offers a quieter and more reflective experience compared to the bustling major sites.

How to Get There: The temple is situated in Qurna, a village on the West Bank. It can be reached by taxi or as part of a specialized West Bank tour.

Address: Temple of Seti I, Qurna, West Bank, Luxor, Egypt

Hours of Operation: Typically open from 6:00 AM to 5:00 PM. Check in advance for any seasonal changes in hours.

Admission: Tickets are purchased on-site. It's advisable to confirm ticket availability and prices locally.

2. Ramesseum

The Ramesseum is a lesser-known temple dedicated to Ramses II, located on the West Bank. The temple complex includes impressive statues, a large mortuary temple, and well-preserved reliefs depicting Ramses II's victories. It offers a more peaceful experience compared to the more frequented sites.

How to Get There: Situated near the Valley of the Kings, the Ramesseum is accessible by taxi or as part of a West Bank tour. It is located close to other major sites, making it an easy addition to a day of exploration.

Address: Ramesseum, West Bank, Luxor, Egypt

Hours of Operation: Generally open from 6:00 AM to 5:00 PM. Verify hours in advance.

Admission: Tickets can be purchased on-site. Consider a combined ticket for access to multiple West Bank attractions.

Local Markets and Crafts

1. El-Tanoura Market

El-Tanoura Market is a bustling local market in Luxor where visitors can experience daily Egyptian life. The market offers a variety of local products, including fresh produce, spices, textiles, and handcrafted goods. It's a great place to find unique souvenirs and immerse yourself in the local culture.

How to Get There: Located in the city center, El-Tanoura Market is easily accessible by walking or taxi from most central hotels.

Address: El-Tanoura Market, Luxor, Egypt

Hours of Operation: Open daily, usually from morning until late afternoon. Hours may vary depending on the day and season.

Admission: Free to enter. Costs will depend on purchases made at the market.

2. Luxor's Artisan Village

Luxor's Artisan Village is a hidden gem where visitors can see traditional Egyptian crafts being made. The village showcases a variety of handcrafted goods, including pottery, jewelry, and textiles. It provides an opportunity to purchase unique items directly from local artisans and observe traditional crafting techniques.

How to Get There: The Artisan Village is located on the West Bank, near the Valley of the Kings. It can be reached by taxi or as part of a specialized tour.

Address: Artisan Village, West Bank, Luxor, Egypt

Hours of Operation: Typically open from 9:00 AM to 6:00 PM. Check locally for specific hours.

Admission: Free to enter. Costs are based on purchases of handcrafted items.

3. Karnak Village Souk

The Karnak Village Souk is a vibrant local market situated near the Karnak Temple. It offers a range of traditional Egyptian goods, including textiles, spices, and souvenirs. The souk is less touristy compared to other markets, providing a more authentic shopping experience.

How to Get There: Located near Karnak Temple, it is accessible by walking or a short taxi ride from central Luxor.

Address: Karnak Village Souk, Karnak, Luxor, Egypt

Hours of Operation: Open daily, typically from morning until evening. Hours may vary.

Admission: Free to enter. Purchases will vary based on what is bought from the vendors.

Scenic Spots and Natural Wonders in Luxor

Luxor's natural beauty and scenic landscapes offer a variety of experiences that complement the city's rich historical sites. Here are some of the most remarkable natural wonders and scenic spots to explore:

1. The Nile River

The Nile River, the lifeblood of Egypt, is a stunning feature of Luxor. Taking a cruise along the river offers breathtaking views of the lush green banks contrasted with the surrounding desert landscape. A felucca ride, a traditional Egyptian sailboat, provides a serene and picturesque experience as you glide past ancient temples, rural villages, and the mesmerizing sunset.

How to Get There:
The Nile River runs through Luxor, and river cruises can be arranged from various docks along the riverfront. Felucca rides can be booked from the Corniche or through local tour operators.

Address: Nile River, Luxor, Egypt

Contact Information:
For felucca rides, contact local boat operators along the Corniche or book through a tour company. Major cruise operators can be contacted via their offices in Luxor.

Hours of Operation: Felucca rides and river cruises are typically available from early morning until sunset. Check with operators for specific timing.

Admission: Varies by cruise or ride. Felucca rides are usually negotiable, while river cruises have set prices.

2. Theban Hills

The Theban Hills, located on the West Bank, offer dramatic views of the ancient tombs and temples nestled within the rocky terrain. The hills provide a vantage point for stunning panoramic views of the surrounding landscape, including the Valley of the Kings and the Nile River.

How to Get There:
Accessible by taxi or as part of a guided tour. The hills can be explored as part of a West Bank itinerary.

Address: Theban Hills, West Bank, Luxor, Egypt

Hours of Operation The area is accessible during daylight hours. Guided tours often visit in the morning to avoid the heat.

Admission: There is no specific admission fee for the hills. Costs may be associated with guided tours.

3. Luxor's Botanical Garden

Located on the West Bank, Luxor's Botanical Garden is a tranquil oasis filled with exotic plants, trees, and flowers. This lush garden provides a peaceful retreat from the city's bustling streets and offers beautiful views of the surrounding landscape.

How to Get There:
The Botanical Garden is located on the West Bank. It can be accessed by taxi or as part of a tour that includes visits to other West Bank sites.

Address: Botanical Garden, West Bank, Luxor, Egypt

Hours of Operation: Typically open from 8:00 AM to 5:00 PM. Check locally for any seasonal changes in hours.

Admission: Fees are usually modest. Verify current rates on-site or with local guides.

Unique Experiences and Activities in Luxor

Luxor offers a variety of unique experiences that allow visitors to engage deeply with both its ancient heritage and contemporary culture. Here are some activities to consider:

1. Hot Air Balloon Ride

A hot air balloon ride over Luxor provides an unparalleled view of the city's ancient monuments, temples, and the stunning Nile River. The early morning flights offer a magical experience as the sun rises over the horizon, casting a golden glow over the landscape.

How to Get There: Balloon rides depart from the West Bank, near the Nile. Pickup and drop-off services are usually provided by balloon companies.

Address: Hot Air Balloon Launch Sites, West Bank, Luxor, Egypt

Contact Information:
Various operators offer balloon rides, including:
- **Ballooning Egypt:** +20 95 237 4458
- **Sky Cruise:** +20 95 237 6570

Hours of Operation: Balloon rides are typically scheduled for early morning flights, just before sunrise.

Admission: Prices vary by operator. Booking in advance is recommended.

2. Nubian Village Visit

A visit to a Nubian village provides a unique cultural experience. Nubian villages are known for their colorful houses, traditional crafts, and warm hospitality. Visitors can experience local customs, enjoy traditional Nubian cuisine, and learn about the rich heritage of the Nubian people.

How to Get There:
Nubian villages are accessible by boat from Luxor or by road. Tours to Nubian villages can be arranged through local operators.

Address: Nubian Villages, around Lake Nasser, accessible from Luxor

Contact Information:
- Nubian Adventures: +20 95 237 2789

Hours of Operation: Tours are usually arranged for daytime visits. Check with tour operators for specific timings.

Admission: Costs vary based on the tour package. Booking through a tour operator is recommended.

3. Sunset Desert Safari

A desert safari near Luxor offers an exhilarating experience through the sands surrounding the city. Safaris typically include dune bashing, camel rides, and a chance to watch the sunset over the vast desert landscape.

How to Get There:
Desert safari tours can be booked through local operators, who will provide transportation to and from the desert areas.

Address: Desert Safari Areas, outside Luxor city center

Contact Information:
- **Desert Safari Luxor: +20 95 238 5110**

Hours of Operation: Safaris are generally conducted in the late afternoon and evening to coincide with sunset.

Admission: Fees vary based on the tour package and inclusions. Booking in advance is recommended.

4. Egyptian Cooking Class

An Egyptian cooking class offers a hands-on experience in preparing traditional Egyptian dishes. Classes typically include a market visit to select fresh ingredients, followed by a cooking session where participants learn to make dishes like koshari and falafel.

How to Get There: Cooking classes can be arranged through local culinary schools or tour operators. Many classes are held in private homes or dedicated cooking facilities.

Address:
Various locations in Luxor

Contact Information:
- **Luxor Cooking School: +20 95 237 9934**

Hours of Operation: Classes are generally scheduled during the day. Contact providers for specific times and availability.

Admission: Prices vary based on the class and included meals. Booking in advance is recommended.

CHAPTER SIX
Practical Information and Travel Tips

Banks and Currency Exchange in Luxor
Luxor, a major tourist destination, offers various banking and currency exchange facilities to cater to both locals and visitors. Here's a comprehensive guide to managing your finances while in Luxor:

1. Major Banks

National Bank of Egypt (NBE)
The National Bank of Egypt is one of the largest and oldest banks in the country, offering a wide range of banking services including currency exchange, savings accounts, and ATM services.
Address:
- **National Bank of Egypt, Khaled Ibn El Walid Street, Luxor, Egypt**

Contact Information:
- **Phone: +20 95 237 4845**

73

Hours of Operation: Typically open from 8:30 AM to 3:00 PM, Sunday through Thursday. Closed on Fridays and Saturdays.

2. Banque Misr

Banque Misr provides comprehensive banking services, including currency exchange and ATM facilities. It is well-known for its customer service and availability of foreign currency.

Address: Banque Misr, Tahrir Street, Luxor, Egypt
Contact Information:
- **Phone: +20 95 237 7111**

Hours of Operation: Generally open from 8:30 AM to 3:00 PM, Sunday through Thursday. Closed on Fridays and Saturdays.

3. Cairo Bank

Cairo Bank offers various banking services such as currency exchange, savings accounts, and ATM access. It is a convenient option for tourists needing financial services.

Address: Cairo Bank, Corniche El-Nil, Luxor, Egypt

Contact Information:

- Phone: +20 95 238 4500

Hours of Operation: Open from 8:30 AM to 3:00 PM, Sunday through Thursday. Closed on Fridays and Saturdays.

Currency Exchange

Currency exchange services are available at banks, as well as at specialized exchange bureaus and some hotels. For the best rates and convenience, consider using banks or dedicated exchange bureaus.

1. Luxor Exchange Bureau

Luxor Exchange Bureau provides currency exchange services with competitive rates. It is a reliable option for exchanging cash and travelers' checks.

Address: Luxor Exchange Bureau, Main Street, Luxor, Egypt

Contact Information:
- Phone: +20 95 237 8090

Hours of Operation:

Typically open from 9:00 AM to 6:00 PM, Monday through Saturday. Closed on Sundays.

2. Hotel Currency Exchange

Many hotels in Luxor offer currency exchange services for guests. While convenient, hotel exchange rates may not always be as favorable as those at banks or exchange bureaus.

Hours of Operation:
Varies by hotel. Generally available during hotel reception hours.

ATMs and Credit Card Usage

ATMs

ATMs are widely available in Luxor and are often located near banks, shopping centers, and major hotels. They provide a convenient way to withdraw local currency. Most ATMs accept international credit and debit cards.

1. **National Bank of Egypt ATMs**
Location: Various locations throughout Luxor, including near major tourist areas.

2. **Banque Misr ATMs**
Located in and around Luxor city center, including near shopping areas and banks.

3. **Cairo Bank ATMs**

Location: Available in key areas of Luxor, including near the Corniche and other central locations.

Credit Card Usage

Credit cards are widely accepted in hotels, restaurants, and shops, especially in more tourist-oriented establishments. However, smaller businesses and local markets may prefer cash. It's a good idea to carry some cash for transactions where cards are not accepted.

Emergency Contacts and Services
1. Emergency Services

Police:
- Phone: +20 95 237 7744

Ambulance:
- Phone: +20 95 238 1030

Fire Department:
- Phone: +20 95 237 9911

2. Local Hospitals

Luxor International Hospital
A major hospital in Luxor providing comprehensive medical services, including emergency care.

Address: **Luxor International Hospital, Karnak Road, Luxor, Egypt**

Contact Information:
- Phone: +20 95 237 8888

3. Private Clinics
Luxor Private Clinic
Offers general medical services and emergency care. Suitable for minor health issues and consultations.

Address: **Luxor Private Clinic, El-Tahrir Street, Luxor, Egypt**

Contact Information:
- Phone: +20 95 237 2222

4. Tourist Police
Dedicated to assisting tourists with any issues or concerns during their visit.

Address: Luxor Tourist Police Station, Corniche El-Nil, Luxor, Egypt

Contact Information:
- Phone: +20 95 237 3333

Local Laws and Regulations in Luxor

Understanding local laws and regulations is crucial for a trouble-free visit to Luxor. Here's an overview of key legal aspects to be aware of:

1. Dress Code and Behavior
Dress Code: While Luxor is relatively liberal compared to some other parts of Egypt, modest dress is recommended, especially when visiting religious or historical sites. Avoid wearing revealing clothing.

Behavior: Public displays of affection are discouraged. Respect local customs and traditions, particularly in more conservative areas.

2. Drug Laws

Drug Restrictions: Egypt has strict drug laws. Possession of even small amounts of illegal substances can lead to severe penalties, including imprisonment. Always ensure any medications you bring are prescribed by a doctor and are accompanied by appropriate documentation.

3. Photography Restrictions

Photography: While photography is generally permitted at most tourist sites, certain areas, particularly within military zones or specific government buildings, may have restrictions. Always seek permission before photographing people, especially in rural or conservative areas.

4. Smoking Regulations

Smoking: Smoking is prohibited in many public indoor spaces, including restaurants and public transport. Designated smoking areas are usually provided.

5. Environmental Regulations
Littering: Dispose of trash responsibly. Littering in public places can result in fines. Many tourist areas have designated bins for waste disposal.

6. Alcohol Consumption
Alcohol Laws: Alcohol is available in hotels, restaurants, and bars catering to tourists. Public intoxication is frowned upon, and consuming alcohol in public places outside licensed premises is illegal.

Health Services and Medical Facilities in Luxor

1. Local Healthcare Facilities

Luxor International Hospital
Description: A major hospital providing a wide range of medical services, including emergency care, surgery, and general healthcare.
- **Address: Karnak Road, Luxor, Egypt**
- **Contact Information: Phone: +20 95 237 8888**

Luxor Private Clinic

Description: Offers general medical services and consultations for minor health issues and emergencies.
- **Address:** El-Tahrir Street, Luxor, Egypt
- **Contact Information:** Phone: +20 95 237 2222

2. Pharmacies

Local Pharmacies
Description: Pharmacies are widely available in Luxor, providing prescription medications and over-the-counter drugs. Many pharmacies also offer basic medical supplies.
Hours of Operation: Typically open from 9:00 AM to 9:00 PM. Some may be open 24 hours.

3. Travel Health Services

Travel Clinics
Description: Travel clinics provide health advice and vaccinations for travelers. It's advisable to visit a clinic before traveling to receive advice on necessary vaccinations and health precautions.
Address: Various locations, contact local tour operators for recommendations.

4. Health Insurance
Travel Insurance: Ensure you have comprehensive travel insurance that covers medical expenses abroad. Verify that your policy covers evacuation and treatment for emergencies.

Safety and Security Advice

1. General Safety Tips
Personal Safety: Keep an eye on your belongings and be cautious of pickpockets, especially in crowded areas. Use hotel safes for valuables.
Local Laws: Familiarize yourself with local laws and customs to avoid inadvertently breaking the law.

2. Avoiding Scams
Common Scams: Be wary of offers that seem too good to be true, particularly from unofficial tour guides or street vendors. Always verify the legitimacy of services and prices before making commitments.

3. Emergency Services
Emergency Contacts: Keep a list of emergency contacts, including local police, medical facilities, and your embassy. Emergency numbers include:

- Police: +20 95 237 7744
- Ambulance: +20 95 238 1030
- Fire Department: +20 95 237 9911

4. Natural Disasters

Weather Awareness: While Luxor is relatively safe from natural disasters, be aware of seasonal weather conditions and follow any local advisories. During extreme heat, stay hydrated and avoid prolonged exposure to the sun.

5. Tourist Police

Assistance: Tourist police are available to assist visitors with any issues or concerns. They can provide guidance and support in case of emergencies or if you need help navigating local regulations.

6. Political Stability

Current Situation: Check for any travel advisories or warnings from your government before traveling. Luxor is generally safe for tourists, but it's wise to stay informed about the local political situation and follow any travel advisories.

Cultural Sensitivity Tips for Visiting Luxor

Luxor is a city rich in cultural heritage and traditions. To ensure a respectful and enjoyable visit, here are some cultural sensitivity tips:

1. Respect for Local Customs

Dress Modestly: While Luxor is a popular tourist destination, it's important to dress modestly, especially when visiting religious sites. Women should cover their shoulders and knees, and men should avoid wearing shorts.

Behavior: Public displays of affection, such as kissing and hugging, should be kept to a minimum. It's considered respectful to maintain a more reserved demeanor in public.

2. Interaction with Locals

Politeness: Use polite greetings and gestures. Handshakes are common, but avoid shaking hands with women unless they extend their hand first.
Personal Space: Respect personal space and avoid touching people, especially those of the opposite sex, unless you are familiar with them.

3. Photography Etiquette

Permission: Always ask for permission before photographing people, particularly in rural areas or when visiting private homes. Respect "no photography" signs at certain sites and museums.
Sacred Sites: Be especially cautious when taking photos in religious or sacred sites. Follow any guidelines provided by the site's management.

4. Dining and Eating

Eating Etiquette: When invited to someone's home, it is customary to remove your shoes before entering. Use your right hand for eating, as the left hand is considered impolite in many contexts.
Tipping: Tipping is customary in Egypt, and it is appreciated to leave a small tip for service staff, such as waiters and hotel staff.

5. Religious Sensitivities

Prayer Times: Be aware of prayer times and avoid disturbing those who are praying. Respect the peaceful environment in mosques and other religious spaces.
Ramadan: During Ramadan, it is respectful to refrain from eating, drinking, or smoking in public during daylight hours. Most restaurants and cafes will be closed during these hours but will open after sunset.

6. Shopping and Bargaining

Bargaining: Bargaining is a common practice in markets and souks. Approach it with a friendly attitude and be prepared for a bit of negotiation.
Respect: If you are not interested in a product, decline politely rather than abruptly.

Essential Phrases in Arabic

Learning a few basic phrases in Arabic can enhance your travel experience and help you connect with locals. Here are some essential phrases:

1. Greetings and Polite Expressions

- Hello: مرحبا (Marhaban)
- Good Morning: صباح الخير (Sabah al-Khayr)
- Good Evening: مساء الخير (Masa' al-Khayr)
- Goodbye: وداعا (Wada'an)
- Please: من فضلك (Min Fadlik)
- Thank You: شكرا (Shukran)
- Yes: نعم (Na'am)
- No: لا (La)

2. Common Questions

- How are you?: كيف حالك؟ (Kayfa Halak?) [to a male] / كيف حالكِ؟ (Kayfa Halik?) [to a female]

- Where is the restroom?: أين الحمام؟ (Ayna al-Hammam?)
- How much does this cost?: كم ثمن هذا؟ (Kam Thaman Hatha?)
- Do you speak English?: هل تتحدث الإنجليزية؟ (Hal Tatahaddath al-Ingliziya?)

3. Emergency Phrases

- Help!: النجدة! (Al-Najda!)
- I need a doctor: أحتاج إلى طبيب (Ahtaj ila Tabeeb)
- I'm lost: أنا ضائع (Ana Da'i)
- Call the police: اتصل بالشرطة (Ittasil bil-Shurta)

Navigating Common Challenges in Luxor

Traveling in Luxor, like any destination, can present some challenges. Here's how to navigate common issues:

1. Language Barrier
Solution: While many people in the tourism industry speak English, learning a few basic Arabic phrases can be very helpful. Use translation apps or carry a phrasebook to assist with communication.

2. Currency Exchange and Payments

Solution: Ensure you have enough local currency for small purchases and transactions. ATMs are widely available, but it's advisable to carry some cash as smaller vendors may not accept cards. Use reputable banks or exchange bureaus for currency conversion.

3. Health and Hygiene

Solution: Drink bottled water and avoid consuming ice or raw foods that may not be prepared under strict hygiene conditions. Carry hand sanitizer and be mindful of food hygiene practices.

4. Navigating the City

Solution: Use reliable transportation options such as official taxis or ride-sharing services. Familiarize yourself with the layout of the city and major landmarks to make navigation easier.

5. Tourist Scams

Solution: Be cautious of offers that seem too good to be true, particularly from unofficial guides or vendors. Always verify prices and services before making commitments. If something feels off, trust your instincts and seek advice from reputable sources.

6. Extreme Weather

Solution: Luxor can be very hot, especially in summer. Stay hydrated, wear sunscreen, and dress in light, breathable clothing. Plan outdoor activities for early morning or late afternoon to avoid the peak heat of the day.

7. Cultural Sensitivity

Solution: Follow local customs and respect cultural practices. When in doubt, observe the behavior of locals and ask for guidance from your hosts or tour guides

CHAPTER SEVEN
Sample Itineraries and Useful Contacts

3-Day Adventure Itinerary: Luxor Highlights

Day 1: Discover Ancient Wonders
Morning: Start your adventure with a visit to the Valley of the Kings. Explore the tombs of ancient pharaohs, including the famous Tutankhamun's tomb. Arrive early to beat the crowds and enjoy cooler temperatures.
Late Morning: Head to the Temple of Hatshepsut, dedicated to the female pharaoh. Admire the impressive architecture and the scenic backdrop of the Theban Mountains.
Afternoon: Visit the Colossi of Memnon, two massive statues that once guarded the entrance to a temple. Spend time taking in the scale and historical significance of these ancient statues.
Evening: Return to Luxor city and stroll along the Corniche for a relaxing evening by the Nile River. Enjoy dinner at a riverside restaurant with views of the sunset.

Day 2: Temples and Markets

Morning: Explore Karnak Temple, one of the largest religious complexes in the world. Spend time wandering through its vast courtyards, monumental pillars, and the Hypostyle Hall.

Late Morning: Visit Luxor Temple, located in the heart of the city. This temple is renowned for its beautiful evening illumination and is a testament to the grandeur of ancient Egyptian architecture.

Afternoon: Discover Luxor's local markets. Visit the Souq and pick up souvenirs, local crafts, and spices. Take time to engage with local vendors and experience the vibrant market atmosphere.

Evening: Enjoy a traditional Egyptian meal at a local restaurant, sampling dishes like koshari or falafel.

Day 3: Nile River and Relaxation

Morning: Experience a hot air balloon ride over Luxor for a breathtaking aerial view of the city and its surroundings. The ride typically starts before sunrise and offers stunning views of the Nile and ancient monuments.

Late Morning: After your balloon ride, relax at one of Luxor's botanical gardens or enjoy a leisurely boat ride on the Nile River in a felucca, a traditional sailboat.

Afternoon: Visit a local spa for a relaxing massage or traditional Egyptian spa treatment.

Evening: Wrap up your trip with a sunset dinner cruise on the Nile River. Enjoy a meal while cruising and take in the scenic beauty of Luxor's illuminated temples and monuments.

5-Day Cultural Exploration: In-Depth Luxor Experience

Day 1: Classic Luxor Sites
- **Morning:** Visit the Valley of the Kings and explore a selection of tombs. Take time to appreciate the intricate artwork and historical significance of these burial sites.
- **Afternoon:** Head to the Temple of Hatshepsut. Explore its terraced structure and learn about its fascinating history.
- **Evening:** Walk around Luxor Temple and marvel at its evening illumination. Enjoy dinner at a local restaurant featuring Egyptian cuisine.

Day 2: Karnak and Ancient Egypt
- **Morning:** Spend the day exploring Karnak Temple. Focus on the Great Hypostyle Hall, the Obelisk of Hatshepsut, and the Sacred Lake.

- **Afternoon:** Visit the Luxor Museum to see a collection of artifacts from ancient Thebes, including statues, mummies, and historical relics.
- **Evening:** Take a leisurely stroll along the Corniche and enjoy a relaxing dinner by the Nile River.

Day 3: West Bank Wonders
- **Morning:** Start with a visit to the Colossi of Memnon, followed by a trip to the Temple of Medinet Habu. This temple is known for its well-preserved reliefs and massive walls.
- **Afternoon:** Explore the Ramesseum, the memorial temple of Ramses II, known for its impressive colossi and detailed inscriptions.
- **Evening:** Enjoy a traditional Egyptian dinner and attend a cultural performance, such as a dance or music show.

Day 4: Market and Village Life
- **Morning:** Visit a Nubian village to experience local culture. Explore the colorful homes, interact with residents, and learn about Nubian traditions.
- **Afternoon:** Return to Luxor and explore local markets. Spend time shopping for souvenirs and handicrafts, and enjoy street food or a light meal at a local café.

- **Evening:** Experience a sunset cruise on the Nile River, taking in the serene views of the river and surrounding landscape.

Day 5: Relaxation and Reflection
- **Morning:** Visit the Temple of Luxor and take a guided tour to understand its historical and cultural significance.
- **Afternoon:** Relax at one of Luxor's botanical gardens or spend some time at a spa for a rejuvenating experience.
- **Evening:** Enjoy a farewell dinner at a fine dining restaurant with views of the Nile, reflecting on your enriching cultural journey through Luxor.

7-Day Ultimate Luxor Experience: Comprehensive Exploration

Day 1: Arrival and Introduction
- **Morning:** Arrive in Luxor and check into your hotel. Take some time to settle in and acclimate to the city.
- **Afternoon:** Visit the Luxor Museum to get an introduction to the region's rich history and artifacts.
- **Evening:** Stroll along the Corniche and enjoy a relaxing dinner by the Nile River.

Day 2: Temple Highlights
- **Morning:** Explore Karnak Temple. Spend time marveling at its monumental structures and vast courtyards.
- **Afternoon:** Visit Luxor Temple and appreciate its historical significance and architectural beauty.
- **Evening:** Enjoy a traditional Egyptian meal and explore local shops or markets.

Day 3: The West Bank Exploration
- **Morning:** Visit the Valley of the Kings and explore several tombs. Continue to the Temple of Hatshepsut and the Colossi of Memnon.

- **Afternoon:** Explore the Temple of Medinet Habu and the Ramesseum.
- **Evening:** Return to Luxor and enjoy a relaxed evening with dinner at a local restaurant.

Day 4: Cultural Immersion
- **Morning:** Experience a hot air balloon ride over Luxor for a breathtaking view of the city and its surroundings.
- **Afternoon:** Visit a Nubian village for a deep dive into local culture. Learn about Nubian traditions, crafts, and cuisine.
- **Evening:** Attend a cultural performance or dance show.

Day 5: Market and Local Life
- **Morning:** Explore Luxor's vibrant markets. Enjoy shopping for souvenirs, crafts, and local products.
- **Afternoon:** Visit a local café for lunch and spend the afternoon relaxing or exploring further.
- **Evening:** Enjoy a dinner cruise on the Nile River, taking in the illuminated temples and the city skyline.

Day 6: Scenic and Relaxation

- **Morning:** Visit the Temple of Luxor and take a guided tour to learn about its historical significance.
- **Afternoon:** Relax at a botanical garden or enjoy a spa treatment. Consider a visit to local art galleries or cultural centers.
- **Evening:** Enjoy a leisurely dinner at a fine dining restaurant with views of the Nile River.

Day 7: Reflection and Departure

Morning: Take a final stroll around Luxor or visit any remaining sites of interest.

Afternoon: Prepare for departure, ensuring you have all your belongings and any last-minute purchases.

Evening: Depart Luxor, reflecting on your comprehensive and enriching experience in this ancient city.

Customizable Itinerary Tips for Luxor

Creating a flexible and personalized itinerary can enhance your travel experience in Luxor. Here are some tips for customizing your itinerary based on your interests and preferences:

1. Prioritize Your Interests

Historical Sites: If you're passionate about history and archaeology, prioritize visits to major temples, tombs, and museums. Focus on landmarks such as Karnak Temple, the Valley of the Kings, and Luxor Temple.

Cultural Experiences: For a deeper cultural immersion, consider exploring local markets, attending cultural performances, and visiting Nubian villages.

Adventure Activities: If you enjoy adventure, include activities like hot air balloon rides, desert safaris, or felucca rides on the Nile.

2. Allow for Flexibility

Adjust Timings: Depending on your pace, adjust the timing of visits to different sites. Allow extra time for exploration or relaxation, and be prepared to modify plans based on weather or local events.

Rest Days: Incorporate rest days into your itinerary to avoid burnout. Use these days to relax at your hotel, enjoy a spa treatment, or explore at a leisurely pace.

3. Mix and Match Activities

Combine Sightseeing with Relaxation: Balance intense sightseeing days with relaxing activities. For example, after a day of exploring temples, enjoy a calming felucca ride or a leisurely evening stroll.
Blend Cultural and Adventure: Mix cultural visits with adventure activities. Combine a trip to a historical site with a visit to a local market or a cultural performance.

4. Plan for Local Events

Check Local Calendars: Look into local festivals, events, or seasonal activities that might be happening during your visit. This could provide unique experiences and enhance your trip.
Book in Advance: For popular events or activities, book tickets or reservations in advance to ensure availability.

5. Consider Travel Preferences

Transportation: Choose transportation options based on your comfort and convenience. Luxor offers taxis, ride-sharing services, and car rentals. Select what best fits your travel style.

Accommodation: Tailor your lodging choices based on your budget and preferences. Luxor offers a range of options from budget hostels to luxury resorts.

Tourist Information Centers in Luxor

Tourist Information Centers provide valuable resources and assistance for visitors. Here's a guide to the main centers in Luxor:

1. Luxor Tourist Information Center

Description: Offers maps, brochures, and advice on local attractions, accommodations, and transportation. Staff can assist with booking tours and providing general information about Luxor.
- **Address:** 3rd Floor, Luxor Hotel, Corniche El-Nil, Luxor, Egypt
- **Contact Information:** Phone: +20 95 237 6050

Hours of Operation: Typically open from 9:00 AM to 5:00 PM, daily.

2. Luxor Museum Visitor Center

Description: Provides information about the Luxor Museum, including exhibition details, ticketing, and guided tour options. Staff can also offer general advice on nearby attractions.
- **Address: Luxor Museum, Corniche El-Nil, Luxor, Egypt**
- **Contact Information: Phone: +20 95 237 1010**

Hours of Operation: Open from 9:00 AM to 7:00 PM, daily.

3. Luxor West Bank Tourist Information

Description: Located on the West Bank, this center focuses on attractions and activities in the West Bank area, including the Valley of the Kings and the Temple of Hatshepsut.
- **Address: West Bank, Luxor, Egypt**
- **Contact Information: Phone: +20 95 238 3020**

Hours of Operation: Open from 8:00 AM to 4:00 PM, daily.

Local Guides and Tour Operators

Local guides and tour operators can enhance your experience by providing expert knowledge and facilitating smooth visits to various attractions. Here's a list of reputable options:

1. Luxor Tours and Travel

Description: Offers a variety of guided tours including historical site visits, cultural experiences, and adventure activities. Personalized itineraries can be arranged based on interests.
Address: Luxor Tours and Travel Office, El-Tahrir Street, Luxor, Egypt
Contact Information: Phone: +20 95 237 8000
Website: luxortours.com
Hours of Operation: Monday to Saturday, 9:00 AM to 6:00 PM.

2. Egypt Travel Guides

Description: Provides comprehensive tours of Luxor and other Egyptian destinations, with options for private and group tours. Services include transportation, entry tickets, and expert guides.

- **Address: Egypt Travel Guides Office, Main Street, Luxor, Egypt**
- **Contact Information: Phone: +20 95 238 5000**
- **Website: egypttravelguides.com**

Hours of Operation: Sunday to Friday, 8:00 AM to 5:00 PM.

3. Nile Valley Tours

Description: Specializes in tailored tours of Luxor and the Nile Valley, including historical sites, cultural experiences, and river cruises. Offers customizable itineraries and luxury options.

- **Address: Nile Valley Tours Office, Karnak Road, Luxor, Egypt**
- **Contact Information: Phone: +20 95 237 9000**
- **Website: nilevalleytours.com**

Hours of Operation: Monday to Saturday, 8:00 AM to 6:00 PM.

4. Discover Egypt

Description: Offers guided tours, package deals, and custom experiences throughout Luxor and Egypt. Focuses on providing in-depth knowledge and a rich cultural experience.

- **Address:** Discover Egypt Office, Corniche El-Nil, Luxor, Egypt
- **Contact Information:** Phone: +20 95 238 4000
- **Website:** discoveregypt.com

Hours of Operation: Sunday to Friday, 9:00 AM to 5:00 PM.

Conclusion

This guide will help you get ready for your trip to Luxor and will open the door to discovering one of Egypt's most fascinating locations. Luxor promises a remarkable experience through its remarkable blend of ancient history, vibrant culture, and natural beauty. It is frequently hailed as the greatest open-air museum in the world.

From the awe-inspiring temples and tombs that echo the grandeur of ancient Egyptian civilization to the bustling markets and serene Nile river cruises, Luxor offers a rich tapestry of experiences that cater to every traveler's interests. Whether you are an avid historian, an adventurous soul, or a cultural enthusiast, the treasures of Luxor are sure to leave a lasting impression.

In crafting your itinerary, remember to balance exploration with relaxation, immerse yourself in the local culture, and remain flexible to embrace the unexpected delights that may arise. Engage with local guides to gain deeper insights into the city's treasures and savor every moment of your adventure.

This guide is designed to equip you with essential information, practical tips, and insightful recommendations to ensure a seamless and enriching travel experience. As you embark on your journey through Luxor, may you uncover the wonders of this ancient city and create memories that will resonate long after you depart.

Luxor awaits with its timeless allure, inviting you to step into a world where history comes alive and every corner reveals a story from the past. Embrace the magic of Luxor, and let your adventure be as grand as the legacies it holds. Safe travels and enjoy the magnificent journey through one of the world's most extraordinary destinations.

Feedback Request

Thank you for choosing **"Luxor Travel Guide 2025"** as your companion for exploring one of Egypt's most historic and captivating destinations. Your feedback is incredibly valuable to me, and I would greatly appreciate it if you could take a moment to leave a review on Amazon. Your insights help other travelers and support the continued creation of guides like this one. Thank you for your time, and I hope you have an unforgettable adventure in Luxor!

TRAVEL

DATE:
DURATION:

DESTINATION:

PLACES TO SEE:
1.
2.
3.
4.
5.
6.
7.

LOCAL FOOD TO TRY:
1.
2.
3.
4.
5.
6.
7.

DAY 1	DAY 2	DAY 3

DAY 4	DAY 5	DAY 6

NOTES

EXPENSES IN TOTAL:

PLANNER

TRAVEL

DATE:
DURATION:

DESTINATION:

PLACES TO SEE:	LOCAL FOOD TO TRY:
1.	1.
2.	2.
3.	3.
4.	4.
5.	5.
6.	6.
7.	7.

DAY 1	DAY 2	DAY 3

DAY 4	DAY 5	DAY 6

NOTES	EXPENSES IN TOTAL:

PLANNER

TRAVEL

DATE: _____
DURATION: _____

DESTINATION: _____

PLACES TO SEE:

1. _____
2. _____
3. _____
4. _____
5. _____
6. _____
7. _____

LOCAL FOOD TO TRY:

1. _____
2. _____
3. _____
4. _____
5. _____
6. _____
7. _____

DAY 1	DAY 2	DAY 3

DAY 4	DAY 5	DAY 6

NOTES

EXPENSES IN TOTAL:

PLANNER

TRAVEL

DATE:
DURATION:

DESTINATION:

PLACES TO SEE:	LOCAL FOOD TO TRY:
1.	1.
2.	2.
3.	3.
4.	4.
5.	5.
6.	6.
7.	7.

DAY 1	DAY 2	DAY 3

DAY 4	DAY 5	DAY 6

NOTES	EXPENSES IN TOTAL:

PLANNER

TRAVEL

DATE:
DURATION:

DESTINATION:

PLACES TO SEE:	LOCAL FOOD TO TRY:
1	1
2	2
3	3
4	4
5	5
6	6
7	7

DAY 1	DAY 2	DAY 3

DAY 4	DAY 5	DAY 6

NOTES	EXPENSES IN TOTAL:

PLANNER

TRAVEL

DATE:
DURATION:

DESTINATION:

PLACES TO SEE:
1.
2.
3.
4.
5.
6.
7.

LOCAL FOOD TO TRY:
1.
2.
3.
4.
5.
6.
7.

DAY 1	DAY 2	DAY 3

DAY 4	DAY 5	DAY 6

NOTES

EXPENSES IN TOTAL:

PLANNER

TRAVEL

DATE:
DURATION:

DESTINATION:

PLACES TO SEE:
1.
2.
3.
4.
5.
6.
7.

LOCAL FOOD TO TRY:
1.
2.
3.
4.
5.
6.
7.

DAY 1	DAY 2	DAY 3

DAY 4	DAY 5	DAY 6

NOTES

EXPENSES IN TOTAL:

PLANNER

TRAVEL

DATE:
DURATION:

DESTINATION:

PLACES TO SEE:
1.
2.
3.
4.
5.
6.
7.

LOCAL FOOD TO TRY:
1.
2.
3.
4.
5.
6.
7.

DAY 1	DAY 2	DAY 3

DAY 4	DAY 5	DAY 6

NOTES

EXPENSES IN TOTAL:

PLANNER

TRAVEL

DATE:
DURATION:

DESTINATION:

PLACES TO SEE:	LOCAL FOOD TO TRY:
1.	1.
2.	2.
3.	3.
4.	4.
5.	5.
6.	6.
7.	7.

DAY 1	DAY 2	DAY 3

DAY 4	DAY 5	DAY 6

NOTES	EXPENSES IN TOTAL:

PLANNER

TRAVEL

DATE:
DURATION:

DESTINATION:

PLACES TO SEE:	LOCAL FOOD TO TRY:
1	1
2	2
3	3
4	4
5	5
6	6
7	7

DAY 1	DAY 2	DAY 3

DAY 4	DAY 5	DAY 6

NOTES	EXPENSES IN TOTAL:

PLANNER

TRAVEL

DATE:
DURATION:

DESTINATION:

PLACES TO SEE:
1.
2.
3.
4.
5.
6.
7.

LOCAL FOOD TO TRY:
1.
2.
3.
4.
5.
6.
7.

DAY 1	DAY 2	DAY 3

DAY 4	DAY 5	DAY 6

NOTES

EXPENSES IN TOTAL:

PLANNER

Printed in Great Britain
by Amazon